DOPAMINE TRAP: HOW SOCIAL MEDIA HIJACKS YOUR MIND

The Hidden Cost of Social Media on Your Self-Esteem, Focus, and Happiness

Asa Eccleston-Kibilski

CONTENTS

WELCOME TO THE MATRIX – UNDERSTANDING SOCIAL MEDIA'S GRIP

Imagine stepping into a vast, ever-expanding digital metropolis – its streets buzzing with updates, its shops brimming with eye-catching content, and its central squares teeming with a relentless hum of opinions, arguments, and self-promotion. This is the world of social media, where the currency is attention, the architecture is shaped by algorithms, and the allure of endless connection often disguises a path towards isolation.

In this ebook, we'll venture beyond the brightly lit facades of social platforms to explore their profound psychological, social, and even economic impact. You'll uncover the ingenious mechanisms these platforms use to keep you scrolling, liking, and sharing – often at the expense of your mental health, privacy, and well-being. It's a journey that will challenge your perceptions and, perhaps, inspire you to alter your relationship with the digital realm.

The Goal: From Mindless Consumer to Mindful User

This isn't a manifesto against social media. These platforms offer benefits – connection, self-expression, access to information, and even entertainment. However, unchecked and uncritical use can leave us feeling drained, anxious, insecure, and tethered to a never-ending stream of manufactured outrage, idealized lives, and divisive content.

The aim of this ebook is to illuminate the hidden forces at play behind your screen, to peel back the curtain on the attention economy, and to empower you to transform from a passive consumer of content to a conscious, intentional user of technology. We will explore:

- **The Psychological Hook:** How social media exploits our evolutionary wiring, fuels the comparison trap, and hijacks our natural reward systems.
- **Privacy Under Siege:** What happens to the vast amounts of data collected about you, and how it can be used to influence not just what you buy, but potentially who you vote for.
- **The Illusion of Connection:** Can social media deepen genuine human bonds, or do curated posts and endless scrolling ultimately erode real-world social skills and exacerbate feelings of loneliness?
- **Digital Dopamine Traps:** The battle for your attention, and how a simple "like" can feed into addictive patterns that undermine your focus and well-being.

Understanding is Power

Knowledge is the first step towards regaining control. By delving into the science behind social media's influence, you'll gain the tools to identify your own vulnerabilities, recognize the manipulation techniques, and cultivate healthy digital habits. This awareness unlocks the power of choice.

Think of this ebook as your field guide to navigating the social media landscape. It won't provide easy solutions, but rather a nuanced understanding of the challenges, the trade-offs, and the potential pathways to a more balanced, empowered relationship with technology.

Ready to step behind the scenes? Let's dive in.

THE SLOT MACHINE IN YOUR POCKET

The persistent vibrations against your thigh, the insistent chime of notifications, the almost magnetic pull your fingers feel towards the sleek surface of your phone – these sensations are the hallmarks of our digital era. What lies within that glowing rectangle isn't just a world of information, it's a carefully orchestrated ecosystem of apps, algorithms, and interfaces all vying for a piece of your most precious resource: your attention. Social media, in particular, has mastered the art of keeping you hooked, and the uncomfortable truth is: you're not just the user, you're a vital part of the product.

The Psychology of the Pull

Let's step away from the screen for a moment and consider the allure of the classic slot machine. The flashing lights, the whirling symbols, the intoxicating sound of coins cascading after a win – every element is designed to trigger a powerful sense of anticipation and excitement. The promise of a reward, however uncertain, is enough to keep players glued to their seats, pulling the lever again and again.

Social media platforms operate on a strikingly similar principle. The endless scroll of perfectly curated images, the stream of rapid-fire updates, the satisfying red notification bubbles – they are the digital equivalents of those flashing lights and enticing sounds. Each time you pull down to refresh your feed, you're essentially pulling a virtual lever, hoping for a reward. It might be a witty comment from a friend, a flood of likes on a post, a viral video that makes you laugh out loud, or even the simple distraction from a moment of boredom.

The Dopamine Connection

The key to understanding the irresistible pull of social media lies in a tiny yet potent chemical messenger in our brains: dopamine. This neurotransmitter is intricately involved in our reward system, signaling feelings of pleasure, motivation, and reinforcement. When we engage in activities that deliver a dopamine surge – whether it's eating a delicious meal, achieving a goal, or having a satisfying social interaction – our brains effectively say, "That felt amazing! Let's do that again."

Social media companies have become masters at manipulating this dopamine response. Each like, each comment, each share, delivers a tiny hit of feel-good dopamine, reinforcing the behaviors that led to that sensation. This is not happenstance; it's meticulously designed. The architects of these platforms understand human psychology on a frighteningly deep level, and they use that knowledge to keep you scrolling, tapping, and posting.

Engineered for Uncertainty

The most insidious aspect of social media's addictive pull lies in the unpredictability of the rewards. Just like a gambler can't predict when the slot machine will hit the jackpot, you never know what awaits you when you refresh your feed. Perhaps this time you'll stumble upon a thought-provoking article, a heartwarming photo, or a hilarious meme. Or, there may be nothing particularly engaging. The beauty, from the platform's perspective, lies in the uncertainty.

Our brains are wired to respond intensely to novelty and the unexpected. We crave the thrill of surprise, the rush of discovering something new. Social media exploits this inherent drive, constantly dangling the possibility of a delightful distraction, a validation boost, or a dopamine-rich piece of viral content. It's a gamble, a lottery with your attention as the wager.

You Are the Product

There's an adage in the digital age that goes, "If you're not paying for the product, then you are the product." This rings particularly true with social media. While you might not be shelling out a subscription fee, you are offering something far more valuable – your time, your data, and your behavior patterns. Every interaction, every like, every post you share provides these companies with rich insights into your preferences, your beliefs, and your social connections. This information is then used to target you with tailored advertising, keep you scrolling through carefully curated content, and even influence your emotions and decisions.

Breaking the Cycle

The realization that you're not just engaging with an app, but rather an ecosystem designed to exploit your attention and monetize your behavior, can be incredibly unsettling. The slot machine in your pocket is programmed to win, and its house edge is your time, focus, and ultimately, your well-being. But awareness is the first step towards breaking the cycle, and reclaiming control in this digital landscape is more essential than ever.

THE NEUROSCIENCE
OF CRAVING

The feeling is unmistakable. A restless urge bubbling up from within, a persistent tugging at the corners of your consciousness. Whether it's the desire for another swipe through your newsfeed, a longing to see if there are new notifications, or the compulsion to share just one more update, the craving to engage with social media can be surprisingly powerful. This isn't simply a product of boredom or habit – there are complex neurobiological mechanisms underpinning this persistent, and potentially harmful, desire.

The Brain's Reward Circuitry

At the heart of our understanding of craving lies the brain's reward system. This interconnected network of neural structures is responsible for processing pleasurable experiences, from the satisfaction of a good meal to the joy of social connection. Central to this system is the release of dopamine, that powerhouse neurotransmitter we explored in Chapter 1.

When we engage in activities that activate the reward system, dopamine floods key pathways in the brain. Crucially, this system doesn't discriminate between "natural" rewards like food, intimacy, or a sense of accomplishment, and the artificial rewards offered by social media platforms. Every like, comment, and share can trigger the same dopamine surge, reinforcing the behaviors that led to those hits of pleasure.

Hijacking the System

The brilliance and danger of social media lie in how effectively it exploits the brain's reward circuitry. Unlike natural rewards,

which often involve effort or delayed gratification, social media offers immediate, readily available, and endlessly novel stimuli. This constant bombardment of pleasurable sensations overloads the reward system, potentially leading to a desensitization effect. What once felt satisfying with a few likes now requires hundreds, even thousands, to achieve a similar dopamine boost. The craving intensifies, driving an ever-escalating cycle of social media use.

Furthermore, the unpredictable nature of social rewards mirrors the addictive qualities of gambling. The promise of an entertaining post, a flattering comment, or a flood of validation delivers jolts of dopamine that are all the more potent due to their unpredictability. Our brains, designed to seek out patterns and predict outcomes, become caught in the loop, craving the next hit of that digital reward.

The Amygdala and Emotional Cravings

While the dopamine-driven reward system plays a central role in cravings, other brain regions are also complicit. The amygdala, an almond-shaped structure deep within the brain, is our emotional processing center. It's responsible for detecting threats, processing fear, and attaching emotional significance to experiences.

In the context of social media, the amygdala can play a powerful role in driving cravings. The fear of missing out (FOMO), the anxiety of social rejection, and the need to feel connected and validated – these emotional states can create a powerful sense of urgency, pushing us towards our phones. Even negative interactions, such as seeing posts that make us angry or upset, can activate the amygdala, keeping us hooked in a perverse cycle of negative reinforcement.

The Weakening of Self-Control

As cravings for social media engagement intensify, a critical battle plays out within our brains. The prefrontal cortex, located at the front of the brain, is responsible for rational thought, decision-making, and impulse control. It's the voice of reason that tells us to put down our phones, to focus on other tasks, or to log off for the night.

However, repeated overstimulation of the reward system and the amygdala creates an imbalance in the brain. The craving centers become hyperactive, constantly clamoring for attention, while the prefrontal cortex struggles to exert control. This erosion of self-control makes it incredibly difficult to resist the urge to check our phones, even when we know we should be doing something else.

The Long-Term Consequences

The neuroscience of craving sheds light on why social media can be so persistently addictive, particularly for young, developing brains. Over time, the constant craving for social stimulation and validation can alter the brain's delicate wiring. Neural pathways associated with reward-seeking become strengthened, while those involved in self-regulation may weaken. This imbalance can lead to:

- **Decreased attention span:** Accustomed to the quick hits of social media, the brain can struggle to sustain focus on longer, more demanding tasks.
- **Increased impulsivity:** The weakened prefrontal cortex may lead to rash decision-making and an inability to resist immediate temptations.
- **Heightened anxiety and depression:** The constant social comparison and emotional rollercoaster of social media can take a serious toll on mental health.

Understanding the Craving

The aim of this chapter is not to demonize social media but to empower you with knowledge. By understanding the neuroscience behind the constant pull of newsfeeds and notifications, you can become more mindful of your relationship with these platforms. Recognize that the craving is not merely a desire, but a complex physiological and emotional response orchestrated within your brain. This awareness can be the first step towards regaining a sense of control and making conscious, intentional choices about how, and when, you engage with social media.

INFINITE SCROLL: DESIGNED FOR ADDICTION

If social media platforms were slot machines, the infinite scroll would be the lever, relentlessly beckoning you to keep pulling for another round of digital stimulation. This deceptively simple feature, now a staple of almost every major social platform, has transformed our online experience. However, beneath its seamless and intuitive facade lies a powerful mechanism carefully crafted to maximize engagement and cultivate a type of dependency.

The Illusion of Limitlessness

Picture the social media feeds of the past: a finite collection of updates, posts, and photos. You'd reach the bottom and experience a natural pause, a cue that perhaps it was time to move on. The infinite scroll shattered this concept. As you near the end of the available content, new items are seamlessly loaded, creating the illusion of an endless, ever-replenishing fountain of potential stimulation.

This has several profound implications. First, it eliminates natural stopping cues. There's no built-in moment of pause, no point when you can think, "I've caught up." The scroll stretches on without end, blurring the boundaries between a short break and a hours-long dive down the digital rabbit hole. The sense of limitlessness is both enticing and overwhelming.

Feeding the Craving Machine

The infinite scroll is a brilliant solution to the inherent limitation of social media platforms as they grapple for user attention. With a constantly flowing stream of new content, there's always the possibility of something more engaging, something more satisfying, just one more scroll away. It preys on our natural curiosity and our desire for novelty, tapping into the brain's reward system to fuel an endless loop of seeking more.

Coupled with the unpredictable reward structure of likes, comments, and shares, the infinite scroll fosters a sense of perpetual anticipation. Much like a gambler can't resist pulling the lever one more time, the promise of another interesting post, funny video, or a social reward is enough to keep fingers flicking downwards.

Maximizing Engagement

From the standpoint of the social media companies, the infinite scroll is a goldmine. The longer they can keep you scrolling, the more opportunities they have to serve you advertisements, gather data on your behavior, and shape the content they recommend. As your eyes devour post after post, these platforms collect an astonishing amount of information on your interests, preferences, social circle, and even your emotional state.

Crucially, the infinite scroll allows for constant tailoring of your feed. Algorithms observe your every interaction – how long you linger on a post, what topics catch your attention, the types of videos you watch all the way through. This information is then used to populate your feed with content calculated to be maximally enticing, keeping you engaged for as long as possible. It's a relentless optimization machine driven by the currency of your attention.

The Loss of Time and Presence

We've all experienced the unsettling sensation of "losing" an hour or two to mindless scrolling. The infinite scroll creates a form of time distortion, where minutes bleed into hours without a moment of real awareness. The endless nature of the feed tricks the brain into undervaluing time spent on the platform – after all, what's just one more scroll in the grand scheme of things?

Furthermore, it fractures our attention. The steady stream of notifications and the constant beckoning of the scroll make it difficult to be fully present in other tasks. Even when the phone is set aside, the anticipation of potential updates can create a background hum of distraction, pulling our focus away from work, conversations, or moments of simple enjoyment.

The End of Boredom

While presented as a feature of convenience, the infinite scroll subtly alters our relationship with boredom. Any moment of downtime, the wait in line, the quiet commute, becomes a potential vulnerability - a moment where the smartphone can swiftly swoop in to provide entertainment. This eliminates the opportunities for our minds to wander, daydream, or simply rest - processes essential to creativity, problem-solving, and emotional self-regulation.

Resisting the Scroll

Recognizing the manipulative design behind the infinite scroll is the first step towards regaining control of your time and attention. Practices like mindful scrolling, where you engage with social media with intention and self-awareness, can help break its addictive hold. Don't underestimate the value of boredom, and be wary of filling every spare moment with a swipe on your phone. The rewards of a less plugged-in life – increased focus, presence, and creativity – might surprise you.

THE "LIKE" BUTTON: A
SHOT OF APPROVAL

In the vast digital landscape of social media, the "like" button stands as a seemingly innocuous icon. A simple thumbs-up, a heart, a smiling emoji – these tiny symbols carry a surprising weight, shaping our online interactions and subtly influencing our self-worth. Yet, behind this seemingly harmless feature lies a complex manipulation of human psychology, fueling social validation loops and potentially leading to a dependence on external approval.

The Social Currency

Likes, at their core, are units of social currency. They represent a quantifiable expression of approval, whether it's a sign of agreement, amusement, support, or simply acknowledgment. With each tap of approval, the poster of the liked content receives a small hit of validation. This act isn't simply passive; it carries a sense of social engagement, a way of saying "I see you, I acknowledge you, and I approve."

On the surface, this seems harmless, even beneficial. Humans are social creatures, and positive feedback helps strengthen bonds and create a sense of belonging within communities, both online and offline. However, when this system of social approval becomes amplified and distorted by the mechanics of social media, it can begin to have a profound impact on our sense of self.

The Science of Validation

Our brains are wired to crave social approval. From an evolutionary standpoint, belonging to a group and being accepted by our peers was essential for survival and reproduction. As such, our brain's reward system releases a burst of dopamine when we experience social acceptance. This positive reinforcement encourages repetition of the behaviors that led to those feelings of pleasure.

Social media platforms, armed with the knowledge of how our brains work, have meticulously designed the like button to capitalize on this deep-seated need for validation. With each notification of a new like, we experience a miniature version of that primal reward response. Our brains interpret these likes as signals of our social worthiness, leading to momentary feelings of satisfaction and even a boost in self-esteem.

The Downside of Quantified Approval

The problem arises when we begin to equate our self-worth with the number of likes we receive. Social media creates a hyper-quantified environment where popularity and approval are reduced to a numerical metric. The more likes, the more desirable, valuable, or successful we appear – at least, that's the distorted signal the brain can receive.

This relentless quest for likes can have several negative consequences:

- **Social Comparison Trap:** Social media makes it incredibly easy to compare ourselves to others on a constant, often curated, basis. When we see others receiving more likes, it can lead to feelings of inadequacy, jealousy, and a diminished sense of self.
- **Performative Posting:** When the value of content becomes tied to its like count, it shifts the focus away from genuine self-expression. We begin to tailor our posts, our photos, and our online personas to what we believe will garner maximum approval, rather than sharing our authentic selves.
- **Anxiety and Dependence:** The unpredictable nature of likes, coupled with their impact on our self-esteem, can

lead to a cycle of anxiety and dependence. We feel pressure to constantly check our notifications, worrying about the reception of our posts and becoming overly reliant on external validation.

The Like Economy

It's important to remember that the like button isn't just a benign feature; it's central to the business model of social media platforms. The more likes (and shares, and comments) your content receives, the more visible it becomes within algorithms, maximizing its reach. This, in turn, benefits the platforms by keeping users engaged and creating more opportunities for targeted advertising.

Moreover, the popularity metric fueled by likes is what attracts influencers and brands. Highly liked content is a currency in itself, leading to lucrative sponsorship deals and social clout within the digital sphere.

Breaking the Cycle of Validation

Recognizing the manipulative design behind the pursuit of likes is the first step towards a healthier relationship with social media. Here are some strategies to break free from the validation cycle:

- **Be Mindful of Your Triggers:** Notice how you feel when you post something, when you check your notifications, and when you see others receiving lots of likes. Understanding your emotional responses is key to changing them.
- **Diversify Your Self-Esteem:** Remind yourself that your value is not defined by numbers on a screen. Build your self-worth on your character, abilities, real-life relationships, and accomplishments outside of social media.
- **Post with Authenticity:** Share content that's meaningful to you, even if you don't expect it to go viral. Resist the urge to tailor posts purely for social approval.

The like button, while seemingly simple, is a potent tool with the capacity to shape our behavior, emotions, and self-perception. By becoming aware of its underlying influence, we can start to engage with social media in a more mindful and intentional manner.

FOMO: THE FEAR OF MISSING OUT

In a world overflowing with updates, experiences, and seemingly perfect glimpses into the lives of others, FOMO (Fear of Missing Out) has become the defining anxiety of the social media age. It's the gnawing feeling that everyone else is having more fun, living a better life, or making more meaningful connections than you are. This constant fear fuels compulsive social media use as we desperately try to stay in the loop, avoid feeling left out, and chase the elusive feeling of being where the excitement is.

The Anatomy of FOMO

FOMO isn't merely about missing a specific party or event; it's a pervasive anxiety rooted in a few fundamental human fears:

- **The Fear of Social Exclusion:** Deep down, FOMO taps into our primal fear of being rejected by the tribe. Social media bombards us with idealized images of gatherings, parties, and connections, amplifying a sense that there's a vibrant social world we're not fully a part of.
- **The Fear of Missing Important Information:** In the information age, we worry about falling behind on trends, news, or crucial updates circulating in our social circles. FOMO drives us to refresh social feeds compulsively, lest we miss the next big thing or a critical piece of information.
- **The Fear of Regret:** FOMO creates the illusion of infinite possibilities, and with them come infinite potential regrets. The decision to stay home while scrolling through an event's photos can generate feelings of self-reproach, fueling the belief that we're missing out on pivotal life experiences.

How Social Media Magnifies FOMO

Social media acts as a potent magnifier of FOMO in several insidious ways:

- **Curated Reality:** People primarily share the highlights of their lives, crafting a meticulously curated version of reality. This constant barrage of idealized posts fuels FOMO as we inevitably compare our everyday lives to the filtered best-of moments of others.
- **Unrealistic Expectations:** Witnessing an endless stream of amazing vacations, picture-perfect relationships, and professional achievements skews our perception of what normal life should be. This breeds dissatisfaction with our own experiences, creating the persistent feeling that we're falling short.
- **Always On:** Social media erases the boundaries between downtime and connected time. Even when physically distant, we maintain awareness of all the potential experiences happening elsewhere, making it hard to relax and fully embrace the present moment.

The Consequences of FOMO

Constant FOMO can take a significant toll on our mental and emotional well-being. Studies have linked this phenomenon to:

- **Increased Anxiety and Depression:** Persistent comparison and the feeling of being left out can exacerbate feelings of anxiety and inadequacy, contributing to depressive moods.
- **Compulsive Social Media Use:** FOMO drives endless scrolling and checking, leading to addiction-like behavior as we desperately attempt to stay informed and alleviate our anxieties.
- **Diminished Self-Esteem:** Constantly witnessing others' curated highlights exacerbates self-doubt and creates an unrealistic benchmark against which we judge our own lives.
- **Sleep Deprivation:** Late-night social media binges, driven by the fear of missing out on updates or conversations, disrupt

healthy sleep patterns.

- **Diminished Real-World Experiences:** As we obsess over capturing and sharing our experiences online, FOMO can erode our ability to be fully present and savor them. Life becomes performative rather than truly lived.

Cultivating JOMO (Joy of Missing Out)

The antidote to FOMO isn't to completely disengage from social media, but rather to develop a more mindful and intentional relationship with it. Here are strategies for cultivating JOMO:

- **Practice Self-Awareness:** Notice the times when social media triggers FOMO. Ask yourself: what am I afraid of missing? Am I comparing myself unfavorably? Recognizing these triggers is the first step to counteracting them.
- **Focus on Gratitude:** Shifting your focus towards what you have, rather than what you lack, cultivates contentment and counteracts FOMO-induced dissatisfaction.
- **Set Social Media Boundaries:** Designate tech-free times and zones in your day to disconnect fully. Experiment with social media "fasts" to rebalance your relationship with these platforms.
- **Engage with the Real World:** Prioritize face-to-face interactions, pursue hobbies and passions, and immerse yourself in experiences that can't be filtered or curated.
- **Recognize the Filtered Reality:** Remind yourself that social media showcases a carefully edited highlight reel, not the full complexity of people's lives.

FOMO is a powerful emotion that social media exploits to keep us hooked. By understanding the roots of this anxiety and consciously working to counteract its influence, we can reclaim a sense of contentment in our own lives, even as the digital world buzzes around us. After all, the most important experiences often cannot be captured in a post.

FILTERED REALITIES: THE PERFORMANCE OF LIFE

Social media platforms have transformed how we present ourselves to the world. Once confined to posed portraits or carefully selected snaps in a photo album, our lives are now subject to a constant, meticulous process of curation and filtering. This quest for the picture-perfect online persona can create a profound disconnect between our digital selves and our authentic, often messier, reality, breeding insecurity and taking a toll on our mental well-being.

The Rise of the Digital Persona

With every tap of a filter, every carefully crafted caption, and every consciously posed selfie, we sculpt a digital persona. This is our idealized online representation – the confident, happy, successful, and adventurous version of ourselves we wish to project to the world.

Social media encourages this performance of the self. The architecture of these platforms revolves around displaying our lives for an audience. Profiles, posts, and stories become digital stages where we can star in a carefully curated version of our own reality.

The Tools of Transformation

Modern smartphones and social media apps provide an unprecedented arsenal of tools for enhancing and manipulating our appearance and surroundings. Here's how we filter our reality:

- **Photo Filters:** With a few swipes, we can smooth our skin, brighten our teeth, alter backgrounds, and add visual effects, all in pursuit of flawless images. These filters blur the line between enhancement and outright fabrication.

- **Selective Posting:** We share the highlight reel of our lives: the vacations, the achievements, the celebratory moments. The ordinary, the difficult, and the mundane rarely make the cut, creating a distorted picture of everyday life.
- **Posed Perfection:** We carefully curate our poses and expressions to project confidence and desirability, often at odds with the spontaneous and unguarded moments that fill most of our days.
- **Strategic Captions:** We craft witty sayings, inspirational quotes, and humblebrags to shape how others perceive our life experiences.

The Impact of Filtered Reality

While the curation of a positive online image seems harmless, this persistent performance of life carries several negative consequences:

- **Distorted Self-Perception:** When we constantly compare ourselves to our own idealized digital personas, it can erode our self-esteem. We begin to see our unfiltered selves as lacking, creating a sense of internal dissatisfaction.
- **The Comparison Trap:** Surrounded by a barrage of seemingly perfect lives on social media, it's incredibly easy to slip into the comparison trap, leading to feelings of inadequacy and self-doubt. It's important to remember that everyone has struggles and imperfections that don't make it into their online profiles.
- **Performative Living:** When capturing and sharing experiences becomes paramount, we can lose the ability to be fully present in the moment. Relationships and events are reduced to photo opportunities and potential content, diminishing their intrinsic value and authenticity.
- **Increased Anxiety:** Keeping up the performance of a picture-

perfect life can be exhausting. The pressure to constantly produce shareable content, along with the fear of being judged on our online image, fuels social anxiety and even burnout.

The Case for Authenticity

We don't exist solely in those posed and polished moments. True connection, both with others and ourselves, requires embracing the full spectrum of human experience: joy and sorrow, confidence and doubt, successes and messy imperfections. Here's why being authentic online matters:

- **Stronger Relationships:** Showing vulnerability and sharing genuine moments creates deeper bonds than the endless highlight reel. People are drawn to the real and relatable.
- **Improved Self-Acceptance:** Resisting the urge to compare our real lives to the filtered versions of others helps foster self-compassion and counters insecurities.
- **Greater Mental Well-being:** Letting go of the performance of perfection reduces anxiety and allows for a healthy relationship with social media, prioritizing connection over comparison.

Striking a Balance

The pursuit of an authentic online presence doesn't equate to sharing every raw and unfiltered detail of our lives. It's about finding a balance between crafting a positive space while being mindful of the performative trap. Here are some tips:

- **Embrace Imperfection:** Occasionally share less polished moments, behind-the-scenes glimpses, or struggles. Vulnerability makes us relatable and combats the illusion of perfection.
- **Focus on Connection:** Use social media to foster genuine connections and conversations, rather than simply broadcasting your life updates.
- **Take Digital Breaks:** Regularly step away from screens

to reconnect with real-world experiences, hobbies, and the unfiltered version of yourself.

Social media affords us the unique ability to curate our digital story. Let it be a story that celebrates the highlights, acknowledges the challenges, and embraces the beautifully imperfect reality of being human.

THE COMPARISON TRAP:
YOUR WORST ENEMY

The world of social media is a double-edged sword. It connects us with others while simultaneously fueling a relentless comparison game that can chip away at our self-esteem and well-being. Seemingly harmless scrolling can quickly become a dangerous descent into an endless cycle of comparing our looks, possessions, accomplishments, and life experiences to the filtered and exaggerated versions we see online, leaving us feeling inadequate and dissatisfied.

The Mechanics of Comparison

Social comparison is a natural human tendency. We evaluate ourselves in relation to others to gain insight, set goals, and find inspiration. However, social media warps this process in several profound ways:

- **The Highlight Reel:** We witness a never-ending stream of idealized moments from other people's lives, creating an unrealistic benchmark against which to measure our own. We don't see the struggles, the setbacks, or the ordinary moments that make up the majority of everyone's lives.
- **Upward Comparison:** Social media makes it incredibly easy to compare ourselves to those we perceive as more successful, attractive, or popular. This upward comparison fuels feelings of envy and inadequacy.
- **Constant Accessibility:** Unlike real-life social comparison, the online world is always on. There's a constant stream of potentially envy-inducing content, making it difficult to escape the comparison game.
- **Quantified Comparison:** The likes, comments, and follower

counts associated with social media posts transform social comparison into a numbers game. We easily become obsessed with metrics that we equate to measures of our own worth.

The Dangers of the Comparison Trap

Persistent and pervasive social comparison has the potential to take a profound toll on our well-being, contributing to:

- **Diminished Self-Esteem:** When we constantly compare ourselves to others' seemingly perfect lives, it erodes our sense of self-worth. We internalize the message that we are not successful, attractive, or interesting enough.
- **Increased Anxiety and Depression:** The envy, self-doubt, and dissatisfaction fueled by social comparison can create fertile ground for anxiety disorders and depression. Studies show a strong association between social media use and depressive symptoms.
- **Body Image Dissatisfaction:** Social media inundates us with idealized and often manipulated images of bodies. This constant barrage fosters unrealistic beauty standards and contributes to body image issues and even eating disorders.
- **Wasted Time and Energy:** Engaging in the endless comparison game robs us of precious time and energy that could be directed towards self-improvement, pursuing goals, and cultivating enriching real-world relationships.

Breaking Free from the Trap

Recognizing the comparison trap for what it is – a detrimental distortion fueled by the mechanics of social media – is the first step towards regaining a healthier perspective. Here are some strategies to break free:

- **Mindful Scrolling:** Pay attention to your emotional state while using social media. If you notice feelings of inadequacy or envy creeping in, take a break or shift your focus to more positive and inspiring content.

- **The Reality Check:** Remind yourself constantly that social media is a curated highlight reel. Everyone has flaws and struggles that they don't broadcast online.
- **Focus on Your Own Growth:** Rather than comparing yourself to others, track your own progress. Celebrate small victories and acknowledge your unique journey toward your goals.
- **Cultivate Gratitude:** Regularly reflecting on the good things in your life, big and small, counters the negativity bias and reduces the pull of envy.
- **Limit Social Media Time:** Set boundaries around your social media usage. Consider designated tech-free times, social media "fasts," or app timers to reduce your overall exposure.
- **Unfollow or Mute:** If specific accounts make you feel particularly bad about yourself, don't be afraid to unfollow or mute them. Curate a feed that's inspiring rather than detrimental to your self-esteem.

The Value of Self-Comparison

Healthy self-comparison isn't about comparing yourself to others; it's about comparing yourself to *yourself*. Focus on how far you've come, the challenges you've overcome, and the skills and qualities you've developed. This fosters growth and self-appreciation.

Social media can be a valuable tool for connection, information, and even inspiration. But, it's crucial to recognize its power to fuel the comparison trap. By being mindful of our online consumption and actively promoting a culture of authenticity over perfection, we can use these platforms in ways that enhance rather than diminish our well-being.

CHASING GHOSTS: THE MYTH OF ONLINE POPULARITY

In the digital world, where likes, followers, and retweets hold immense social currency, the pursuit of online popularity can be an intoxicating allure. The promise of virtual validation, a sense of belonging in a vast online community, and the potential for social and financial rewards propels many to chase the elusive ghost of internet fame. However, this pursuit often leads to disillusionment, compromised mental health, and ultimately, a hollow sense of achievement.

The Appeal of Popularity

Since childhood, popularity often equates to social status, acceptance, and influence. Social media amplifies this phenomenon on a global scale, offering the illusion of unlimited reach and the chance to become widely known and admired. Here's what feeds the desire for online popularity:

- **The Validation Rush:** The likes, comments, and shares that acknowledge our posts feel like social rewards. Each notification triggers a dopamine hit, reinforcing the desire to amass even more virtual validation.
- **The Illusion of Community:** A large following can create the perception of belonging to a devoted community. This fulfills the innate human need for connection, even if the relationships remain largely superficial.
- **The Influencer Dream:** Social media stardom has become a lucrative career path. The potential for financial gain, free products, and brand endorsements adds further allure to online fame.
- **Legacy Building:** The internet feels permanent. Some desire

online popularity as a way to build a lasting digital legacy, leaving their mark on the world even after they are gone.

The High Cost of Virtual Fame

While the rewards of online popularity seem tantalizing, the pursuit often exacts a high cost on our well-being:

- **Authenticity vs. Performance:** The pressure to consistently produce engaging content can lead to inauthenticity. We start presenting a manufactured version of ourselves designed to appeal to the masses, rather than showcasing our genuine personalities.
- **The Numbers Obsession:** Constantly tracking followers, likes, and reach can fuel anxiety. Our self-worth becomes tied to these metrics, creating emotional vulnerability every time the numbers dip.
- **The Negativity Trap:** As visibility increases, so does exposure to online negativity. Trolls, harsh criticism, and cyberbullying can chip away at our self-esteem and create a toxic online experience.
- **Erosion of Privacy:** The quest for online fame often comes at the expense of privacy. It requires the deliberate sharing of personal information, eroding the boundaries between our online and offline selves.
- **Burnout and Emptiness:** Keeping up with the demands of content creation, audience engagement, and self-promotion can lead to burnout. Even when coveted popularity is achieved, it often brings a fleeting sense of fulfillment, ultimately leaving us feeling empty and craving more.

The Rise of Micro-Influencers

The pursuit of online fame isn't limited to those chasing millions of followers. The rise of micro-influencers highlights the widespread desire for even localized popularity. Micro-influencers leverage their smaller yet highly engaged online communities to secure brand deals, gain social status, or simply enjoy a taste of digital influence. While potentially less damaging than the quest for massive scale fame, it still taps into the same mechanisms of validation-seeking and curated self-presentation.

Finding True Value

Seeking validation, connection, and even income opportunities online is perfectly understandable in our digital world. However, hinging your self-worth on constantly shifting metrics and the approval of strangers is a recipe for disillusionment. Here's how to find fulfillment outside the popularity contest:

- **Shift the Focus:** Instead of chasing followers, focus on creating content that you're genuinely passionate about, fostering connection with a smaller like-minded community, or using your platform to advocate for causes you believe in.
- **Practice Self-Acceptance:** Base your self-esteem on your internal values, skills, and real-world relationships, rather than social media metrics.
- **Cultivate Offline Connections:** Invest in real-life friendships and communities. Face-to-face interactions provide a depth of connection that online popularity cannot replicate.
- **Set Boundaries:** Limit your time on social media and resist the urge to constantly compare yourself to others.
- **Unfollow Toxicity:** Actively curate a positive feed by unfollowing accounts that promote unrealistic ideals, incite negativity, or trigger feelings of inadequacy.

Popularity, by its very nature, is fleeting. Likes can turn into dislikes, followers can vanish, and viral trends fade. True fulfillment comes from pursuing passions, cultivating meaningful connections, and building a strong foundation of self-worth that doesn't depend on the shifting sands of online validation. Remember, the most important audience is ultimately the one you see in the mirror.

ECHO CHAMBERS: WHEN OPINIONS BECOME FACTS

Social media's promise of a global interconnected community held the inherent possibility of unprecedented exposure to diverse perspectives, the potential for breaking down biases, and building understanding across cultural and ideological divides. However, the reality we've encountered is far more fragmented. Algorithms tailored to maximize engagement, combined with our tendency towards confirmation bias, create digital echo chambers. These self-reinforcing bubbles insulate us from opposing viewpoints, fostering polarization, misinformation, and an erosion of civil discourse.

How Echo Chambers Form

Echo chambers form through subtle manipulation and our own inherent biases. Here's how they trap us:

- **Algorithms at Work:** Social media platforms rely on algorithms to determine the content that appears in our feeds. These algorithms prioritize posts we're likely to agree with, click on, and share, based on our past behavior patterns. This creates a feedback loop, constantly showing us more content aligned with our existing beliefs.
- **Confirmation Bias:** We are naturally drawn to information that confirms our pre-existing opinions and avoids information that challenges them. This selective exposure insulates us from viewpoints that might change our minds.
- **The Homophily Effect:** Online and offline, we tend to associate with like-minded individuals. This reinforces our existing beliefs and limits exposure to differing perspectives.
- **Self-Selection:** Consciously or subconsciously, we often

choose to follow, interact with, and seek out information from sources that align with our existing worldviews.

The Dangers of Echo Chambers

When trapped inside our own echo chambers, several detrimental consequences emerge:

- **Increased Polarization:** Lack of exposure to opposing viewpoints breeds suspicion and distrust of those who hold different opinions. This societal polarization erodes empathy and makes constructive dialogue increasingly difficult.
- **Misinformation Epidemic:** Echo chambers are fertile ground for the spread of fake news, conspiracy theories, and propaganda. When dissenting voices are suppressed and critical thinking erodes, misinformation can take hold as unchallenged fact.
- **Erosion of Critical Thinking:** When we are surrounded by information that supports our existing beliefs, we're less likely to question its validity or seek alternative perspectives. This weakens our ability to engage in nuanced debate and informed decision-making.
- **Rise of Extremism:** Echo chambers can amplify and normalize extreme viewpoints. Insulated from contradictory information and fueled by a sense of emboldened righteousness, fringe opinions can move towards radicalization.

Breaking Free from the Bubble

Recognizing the existence of echo chambers is the first step towards regaining control over the information we consume. Here are some strategies to break out of the bubble:

- **Diversify Your Feed:** Consciously follow reputable news outlets and accounts that represent viewpoints different from your own. Embrace the feeling of healthy discomfort that comes with considering opposing ideas.
- **Fact-Check Your Sources:** Before sharing information,

particularly emotionally charged content, verify its accuracy using reliable fact-checking websites. This helps counter misinformation that flourishes within echo chambers.

- **Expand Your Circle:** Step outside your online comfort zone. Engage respectfully in online discussions with people who hold different views, seeking to understand, rather than simply to debate.
- **Support Independent Journalism:** The proliferation of opinion-driven and hyper-partisan news sources contributes to polarization. Support news outlets that prioritize factually based, unbiased reporting.
- **Be Mindful of Algorithms:** Remember that social media feeds are constantly personalized based on your activity. Periodically search for topics outside your usual interests to gain a broader perspective.

The Importance of Civil Discourse

Rebuilding a shared understanding of facts and re-learning the art of civil discourse is essential for the health of our society. This doesn't mean abandoning our own convictions. It means actively listening to opposing perspectives with empathy, engaging in respectful debate based on evidence, and being willing to change our minds when faced with compelling arguments or new information. This type of critical thinking and open exchange of ideas is how knowledge and progress move forward.

Social media offers the potential to connect us across vast divides, but its algorithmic design and our own inherent biases can lead to insularity and fragmentation. By recognizing the existence of echo chambers and actively taking steps to broaden our perspectives, we can foster a more informed, tolerant, and resilient society.

THE TOXICITY MACHINE: HATE, TROLLS, AND CYBERBULLYING

The internet, with its combination of anonymity, vast reach, and permanence, has created a breeding ground for a particularly insidious form of harm: online toxicity. From hateful comments and trolling to full-fledged cyberbullying campaigns, social media platforms can become weaponized arenas where negativity, abuse, and cruelty thrive. These attacks have devastating consequences for individuals, especially vulnerable young people, and erode the very fabric of a healthy, civil online discourse.

Forms of Online Toxicity

Online toxicity manifests in a variety of harmful ways:

- **Hate Speech:** Attacks directed at individuals or groups based on their race, religion, sexual orientation, gender identity, disability, or other perceived vulnerabilities. Hate speech incites discrimination, prejudice, and even violence.
- **Trolling:** Deliberate posting of inflammatory, offensive, or nonsensical content designed to provoke emotional reactions, derail conversations, or simply sow discord.
- **Cyberbullying:** Repeated and intentional use of electronic communication to intimidate, harass, threaten, or harm another person. Unlike traditional bullying, cyberbullying can follow its victims 24/7 and is often highly public and difficult to erase.
- **Doxing:** The malicious release of private or personally identifying information with the intent to harm, shame, or intimidate the targeted individual.
- **Revenge Porn:** The non consensual distribution of intimate images or videos with the intent to humiliate or harm an ex-

partner, often as an act of revenge or control.

Why Toxicity Thrives Online

Several factors contribute to why toxicity flourishes in the digital realm:

- **The Online Disinhibition Effect:** The anonymity of the internet, coupled with a sense of physical distance, lowers inhibitions for some people. Things they would never say face-to-face are typed with abandon from behind a screen, leading to vicious personal attacks.
- **The Mob Mentality:** Online crowds can quickly escalate aggressive behavior. Trolls and bullies embolden each other, creating a toxic echo chamber of insults and threats that would likely be less severe in isolated interactions.
- **The Permanence of Harm:** Hurtful words or images posted online can spread with wildfire speed and remain archived indefinitely. Victims often relive the pain and humiliation long after the initial attack, making healing exceptionally difficult.
- **Lack of Clear Consequences:** Despite efforts by platforms, regulating hate speech, and holding perpetrators of cyberbullying accountable remains a complex challenge. This lack of clear and consistent consequences emboldens toxic behavior.

The Devastating Impact

The consequences of online toxicity are far-reaching and severe, especially for young people who are still developing mentally and emotionally:

- **Mental Health Crisis:** Victims of cyberbullying and online hate experience higher rates of anxiety, depression, self-harm, and even suicidal ideation.
- **Damaged Reputation:** False information, humiliating content, and public shaming can ruin reputations, impacting educational and career opportunities for victims long into

the future.

- **Fear and Withdrawal:** The relentless barrage of negativity can lead victims to withdraw from social media and online activities, isolating them further and denying them healthy digital interactions.
- **Erosion of Trust:** The prevalence of cyberbullying and online hate erodes trust and breeds a culture of fear in our digital spaces. This makes people more reluctant to speak out and share ideas out of self-preservation.

Strategies for Combating Toxicity

Addressing online toxicity requires a multi-pronged approach involving tech platforms, law enforcement, educators, parents, and ultimately, all of us as digital citizens. Here's how to fight back:

- **Stronger Platform Moderation:** Social media companies need robust and transparent content moderation policies, proactive tools to identify malicious behavior, and clear consequences for those who violate community guidelines.
- **Legal Recourse:** Laws against cyberbullying and clear legal avenues for addressing non consensual sharing of intimate images are critical for holding perpetrators accountable and deterring such harmful acts.
- **Digital Literacy Education:** Integrating critical thinking skills, empathy education, and online ethics into school curriculum from a young age helps foster a generation of responsible digital citizens.
- **Bystander Intervention:** Encouraging those who witness online abuse to speak up and report it disrupts the mob mentality and supports victims.
- **Support for Victims:** Providing easily accessible mental health resources and reporting hotlines for those impacted

by cyberbullying is essential for helping victims heal and regain a sense of agency.

Cultivating a Culture of Kindness

Ultimately, overcoming online toxicity requires a conscious shift towards a culture of digital respect and empathy. Remember, behind every screen, there's a real person with feelings, vulnerabilities, and a life beyond their online presence.

Let's strive to be the positive change we want to see online. Before you post that comment, consider: Is it true, is it necessary, is it kind? Lead by example, spread positivity, and refuse to let the toxicity machine win.

SLEEPLESS NIGHTS: DISRUPTED RHYTHMS

While social media's dangers to our mental well-being are widely discussed, the insidious impact it has on our sleep is often overlooked. The allure of late-night scrolling, the blue light emitted by our screens, and the anxiety-inducing nature of online content can significantly disrupt natural sleep patterns. This leads to a cycle of sleep deprivation with severe consequences on our physical and mental health.

How Social Media Wrecks Your Sleep

Social media disrupts sleep in several ways:

- **The Blue Light Effect:** The blue light emitted by electronic devices suppresses the production of melatonin, a crucial hormone that regulates our sleep-wake cycle. Exposure to blue light before bed makes it harder to fall asleep and can diminish sleep quality.
- **The Stimulation Trap:** Browsing social media, with its stream of engaging content and notifications, keeps our minds active and alert. This makes it difficult to achieve the mental stillness and relaxation needed to transition into sleep.
- **Delayed Circadian Rhythm:** Using social media late into the night delays our natural circadian rhythm (our internal body clock). This confuses the brain into believing it should stay awake longer and resets the natural sleep schedule.
- **FOMO-Induced Anxiety:** The fear of missing out can trigger restless sleep as we worry about potential updates, interactions, or news developing while we're offline. Social comparison can also provoke anxiety, further fueling

sleeplessness.

- **Doom Scrolling Addiction:** The habit of scrolling through a steady stream of negative news, arguments, or distressing content before bed creates a background state of anxiety and stress, making a restful sleep nearly impossible.

The Consequences of Sleep Deprivation

Sleep deprivation due to social media is a serious health hazard causing a ripple effect of problems:

- **Cognitive Decline:** Lack of sleep impairs focus, memory, problem-solving, and decision-making abilities. Chronic sleep deprivation has been linked to cognitive impairments similar to those seen in aging or intoxication.
- **Weakened Immune System:** Sleep plays a vital role in immune function. When sleep is compromised, the body's ability to fight off infections and recover from illnesses is reduced.
- **Increased Health Risks:** Sleep deprivation is associated with an increased risk of serious health conditions like diabetes, obesity, heart disease, and high blood pressure.
- **Heightened Depression and Anxiety:** Sleep disturbances and mental health disorders are intricately linked. Sleep deprivation can exacerbate symptoms of depression and anxiety, further perpetuating the cycle of sleepless nights.
- **Compromised Daytime Functioning:** Sleep loss leads to drowsiness, irritability, difficulty concentrating, and a greater risk of accidents and errors in school, work, or while driving.

Restoring Sleep Hygiene

Taking back control of your sleep requires adopting healthy sleep habits and limiting social media's disruptive influence:

- **Digital Sunset:** Establish a tech-free period several hours before bed. Power down devices or switch them to "night mode" to reduce blue light exposure. The gradual dimming of lights sends cues to your brain to start producing melatonin.

- **Unplug the Bedroom:** Resist the temptation to scroll in bed. Keep phones and tablets out of the bedroom or designate your bedroom a purely sleep-focused space.
- **Mindful Winding Down:** Replace late-night social media time with relaxing activities that promote sleepiness: reading a calming book, taking a warm bath, or practicing mindfulness meditation.
- **Consistency is Key:** Maintain a regular sleep schedule, even on weekends, to train your body's internal clock. This helps optimize sleep quality and reduce sleep struggles.
- **Address the Source:** If anxiety caused by social media keeps you up at night, consider taking a social media break. Limiting your consumption of negative or distressing content can also make a world of difference.

The Benefits of Reclaimed Sleep

When you prioritize sleep over social media, you'll quickly experience a range of benefits:

- **Boosted Mood:** Well-rested brains are better equipped to manage emotions, leading to a greater sense of positivity and reduced anxiety or irritability.
- **Sharper Thinking:** Improved sleep enhances focus, memory, creativity, and problem-solving abilities – a significant advantage in school, work, and life in general.
- **Stronger Health:** Getting sufficient sleep supports immune function, reduces the risk of chronic diseases, and contributes to overall physical well-being.
- **Greater Calm:** A well-rested mind is less likely to fall prey to anxiety, rumination, or catastrophic thinking induced by social media.

While social media can be a source of connection and entertainment, it's not worth sacrificing your sleep and overall health. Remember, the quality of your sleep significantly influences the quality of your waking life. Choose sleep – your mind, body, and future self will thank you.

FOCUS FRACTURE: THE LOST ART OF ATTENTION

In an era of infinite digital distractions, our most valuable asset – focused attention – is under constant attack. Social media platforms, designed to compete relentlessly for your time, fragment our concentration into ever-smaller slices. This erosion of the ability to sustain deep focus has profound consequences for our productivity, creativity, and overall well-being.

The Attention Economy

Social media companies thrive within what is often termed the "attention economy." Their business models rely on maximizing the time you spend scrolling, tapping, and engaging with their platforms. To achieve this, they utilize a myriad of tactics:

- **Infinite Feeds:** The never-ending stream of content eliminates natural pause points, encouraging continuous scrolling and minimizing opportunities to disengage.
- **Notifications & Alerts:** Constant pings, flashes, and red bubbles hijack our attention, fracturing our focus and pulling us away from tasks at hand.
- **Personalized Content:** Algorithms track our every move to present increasingly tailored feeds, making it difficult to resist the temptation of "just one more" video, post, or article.
- **Autoplay Features:** Videos that start automatically, seamlessly transitioning into the next, create a passive consumption experience that erodes conscious choice and makes it difficult to step away.

The Cost of Shallow Focus

Our brains are not wired for this constant onslaught of stimuli.

The result is a chronic state of shallow focus where we flit between tasks, struggle to maintain concentration on complex work, and find it increasingly difficult to engage with activities that require sustained attention:

- **Reduced Productivity:** Difficulty focusing translates to taking longer to complete tasks, making more errors, and reduced overall output at work or in academic settings.
- **Impaired Creativity:** Creativity and problem-solving flourish during moments of deep concentration and contemplation. Social media-induced attention fragmentation stifles innovation and the ability to generate original ideas.
- **Lower Quality Thinking:** Without sustained focus, we struggle to absorb complex information, analyze concepts critically, or form nuanced opinions. The result is shallow engagement with ideas and an increased reliance on surface-level content.
- **Increased Stress:** The constant barrage of stimuli and multitasking can lead to feelings of overwhelm, frustration, and a relentless sense of never being caught up.

The Long-Term Consequences

Persistent attention fragmentation isn't simply a temporary inconvenience. Over time, it rewires our brains, diminishing our capacity for deep focus and making us increasingly reliant on quick bursts of externally-driven stimulation:

- **Weakened Cognitive Control:** The prefrontal cortex, crucial for focus and impulse control, becomes depleted when over-stimulated. This makes it harder to resist distractions and prioritize long-term goals over short-term temptations.
- **Dependency on Stimulation:** Accustomed to the constant input from social media, our brains may start to find slow-paced or mentally demanding activities less rewarding. This leads to boredom intolerance and further reliance on external sources of distraction.

- **Loss of 'Flow' Experiences:** Flow states – periods of deep immersion in a task where we lose track of time and feel energized and creative – become increasingly elusive. Without these fulfilling experiences, a sense of accomplishment and enjoyment of work is diminished.

Reclaiming Your Focus

Breaking free from the attention traps social media sets requires conscious effort and a commitment to rebuilding your cognitive stamina. Here are strategies to achieve this:

- **Unplug Regularly:** Schedule tech-free time blocks throughout your day. Start small and gradually work towards longer periods where you're fully disconnected from social media, notifications, and even the internet as a whole.
- **Single-task:** Train your brain to focus on one task at a time. Turn off notifications on your phone and close extraneous tabs on your computer. Resist the urge to multitask as it ultimately erodes efficiency.
- **The Pomodoro Technique:** Work in focused 25-minute blocks followed by short breaks. This creates a rhythm and staves off burnout. During breaks, move your body or engage in relaxing activities – avoid reaching for your phone.
- **Embrace Boredom:** Resist the urge to fill every spare moment with digital stimulation. Practice mindfulness during waiting periods or downtime. Allow your mind to wander – this is where creativity and insight often emerge.
- **Curate a Focus-Fueling Environment:** Designate a distraction-free workspace where your phone is out of sight. Use noise-canceling headphones if necessary and consider apps that temporarily block access to distracting websites.

Re-discovering the Joy of Deep Work

As you begin to free yourself from the clutches of the attention economy, you'll re-discover the pleasure and satisfaction that comes from deep work. It may initially feel challenging, but the more you exercise your focus muscle, the stronger it will become. Here's what awaits you with enhanced focus:

- **Greater Efficiency and Productivity:** The ability to concentrate fully on one task allows you to accomplish more in less time.
- **Fulfillment and Flow:** Immersing yourself in challenging work fosters flow states, leading to feelings of accomplishment and enjoyment.
- **Original Thinking:** Deep focus opens the door to unique insights, creative solutions, and genuine innovation.
- **Reduced Stress:** Single-tasking and minimizing distractions leads to a greater sense of control and a calmer mind.

In today's world, protecting your attention is an act of self-preservation. By recognizing the forces competing for your focus and taking active steps to protect it, you safeguard your productivity, creativity, and overall well-being.

THE ANXIETY SPIRAL: DOOMSCROLLING DISTRESS

The term "doomscrolling" has become a modern colloquialism, perfectly capturing the phenomenon of sinking helplessly into an endless stream of negative news, social media feeds teeming with outrage, and distressing content. This compulsive behavior isn't harmless; it fuels a vicious cycle of anxiety and distress, leaving us feeling demoralized, overwhelmed, and pessimistic about the world around us.

Why We Doomscroll

Despite the inherent negativity, there's a strange allure to doomscrolling. Several factors contribute to its powerful grip:

- **The Brain's Negativity Bias:** We have an evolutionary predisposition to focus on potential threats and dangers. Negative news, while distressing, triggers our survival instincts, making it difficult to look away.
- **Morbid Curiosity:** Car accidents, natural disasters, political conflicts – while disturbing, they tap into a morbid fascination that makes them compelling to consume. There's an element of "it could have happened to me" that compels continued engagement.
- **Seeking Validation or Connection:** Doomscrolling about shared crises or social problems can create a sense of distorted community. Bonding with others over negativity can validate our anxieties and offer a warped sense of belonging.
- **Emotional Numbing:** When negativity becomes the norm, we become desensitized. This leads to seeking progressively more shocking or distressing content to feel a sense of

emotional arousal, further deepening the cycle.

- **FOMO Magnified:** In a world plagued by crises, doomscrolling fuels FOMO about the negative. We worry about missing a critical piece of information or an unfolding event, leading to compulsive checking.

The High Cost of Negativity

Doomscrolling may seem like a passive activity, but it comes with serious repercussions:

- **Heightened Anxiety and Depression:** Constant consumption of negative news worsens existing anxiety disorders and contributes to depressive symptoms. It creates a distorted perception of the world, making it seem more threatening and hopeless than it actually is.
- **Diminished Well-being:** Doomscrolling erodes our sense of peace, optimism, and agency. It fosters a sense of helplessness and fuels a cycle of worry that negatively impacts our overall well-being.
- **Distorted Worldview:** News and social media rarely present a balanced picture of reality. Excessive focus on negativity warps our perception, making us underestimate positive events and overestimate risks and dangers.
- **Exacerbated Polarization:** Doomscrolling often involves seeking out information that confirms our existing biases about particular issues or groups. This reinforces our beliefs and hardens our viewpoints, contributing to social divisions and animosity.
- **Lost Time and Productivity:** Doomscrolling is a major time drain; it robs us of precious hours we could use for productive work, hobbies, or meaningful real-life connections.

Breaking the Doomscrolling Habit

Recognizing the detrimental impact of doomscrolling is the first step towards breaking free. Here are strategies to reduce its hold:

- **Set Time Limits:** Use apps that allow you to set time

restrictions for specific social media platforms or news sites. Start small and gradually increase the amount of time you can go without doomscrolling.

- **Curate Your Feed:** Unfollow accounts that consistently post upsetting content, fear-mongering, or outrage-inducing material. Intentionally follow accounts that share positive news, uplifting stories, and inspiring content to balance your feed.
- **Fact-check and Contextualize:** Before spiraling into anxiety based on a headline or social media post, take a step back. Verify the information, look for broader context, and seek out additional reliable sources.
- **The "Good News" Break:** Replace some of your doomscrolling time with deliberately seeking out and consuming positive news stories. Many platforms and news outlets focus on solutions-oriented journalism and uplifting content.
- **Focus on Action:** Channel your negative emotions into constructive action. Get involved in a cause you care about, volunteer, or support organizations working towards positive change. This helps counter the sense of helplessness that doomscrolling fuels.
- **Digital Detox:** Periodically schedule a full digital detox. Leave your phone at home and spend a day immersed in nature, engage in real-world hobbies, and prioritize face-to-face interactions. This helps reset your brain and regain perspective.

Cultivating a Balanced Perspective

Staying informed about current events and social issues is important. However, it's essential to balance your information intake. Remember:

- **The World Isn't Always Ending:** News, by its very nature, focuses on the unusual and dramatic. It rarely reflects the everyday good that fills the lives of most people.

- **Progress Exists:** While crises are real, it's important to remember that human progress, even if slow and uneven, is undeniable. Seek out historical perspectives to counterbalance the constant stream of negativity in the present.
- **You Have Control:** Focus on what you can control: your actions, your responses, and your emotional well-being.

Doomscrolling is a trap our brains fall into easily, especially during times of societal stress and uncertainty. By understanding its mechanisms, curating a healthier relationship with information, and prioritizing emotional well-being, we can resist its pull and foster a more hopeful and empowering view of the world.

SOCIAL ISOLATION: ALONE IN A CROWD

The paradox of social media is that platforms designed to enhance connectivity can, over time, exacerbate feelings of loneliness and social isolation. The curated images of vibrant social lives, combined with superficial interactions and reliance on online communication, can gradually erode our sense of belonging and diminish the quality of our real-world connections.

How Social Media Contributes to Isolation

It's important to emphasize that social media itself doesn't cause isolation directly. However, several factors can contribute to it:

- **The Comparison Trap:** Constantly comparing our own lives to the curated highlights others present online fuels feelings of inadequacy and social disconnection. It creates the illusion that everyone else is happier, more successful, and more socially connected than we are.
- **Superficial Interactions:** While social media facilitates quick interactions and keeping up with acquaintances, it often lacks the depth and intimacy of genuine, face-to-face connection. Numerous "likes" can't replace the support and belonging gained from deep conversations and shared experiences.
- **FOMO's Sting:** Witnessing others' social activity online magnifies FOMO and can create a distorted sense of being excluded. This fuels a drive to "keep up" via social media rather than fostering genuine off-screen connections.
- **Less Face-to-Face Time:** Time spent scrolling displaces time that could be spent engaging in real-world social activities. The ease of virtual interaction reduces motivation to invest

the effort and vulnerability required for deeper, face-to-face relationships.

- **Exacerbating Existing Issues:** For those prone to social anxiety or difficulty developing close bonds, social media can offer a tempting escape rather than a tool to facilitate real connections. Online interaction, while providing some social contact, can reinforce avoidance habits and worsen isolation.

The Dangers of Loneliness

Social isolation isn't just about feeling lonely. It's a recognized public health crisis with serious physical and psychological consequences:

- **Mental Health Decline:** Loneliness is a major risk factor for depression, anxiety, and even suicidal ideation. It increases stress hormones and disrupts sleep, further compounding mental health issues.
- **Physical Health Risks:** Chronic loneliness is associated with higher risk of heart disease, stroke, weakened immunity, and even premature death. These risks are comparable to those posed by smoking and obesity.
- **Cognitive Decline:** Social interaction keeps our brains sharp and engaged. Prolonged isolation can increase the risk of cognitive decline, dementia, and other neurological complications.
- **Vulnerability to Exploitation:** Isolated individuals, especially older adults, are more susceptible to falling victim to scams, manipulation, and online predators.

Breaking Free from the Isolation Loop

If you've noticed social media eroding your sense of connection, take action to reverse the trend. Here's how:

- **Social Media Audit:** Evaluate how using different platforms makes you feel. If any consistently induce comparison or make you feel lonely, unfollow, mute, or reduce your time on them.

- **Intentional Real-Life Investment:** Schedule in-person meetups with friends, join clubs or groups based on your interests, and take classes to expand your social network. Even small interactions like having coffee with a neighbor can go a long way.
- **Face-to-Face Calls:** Instead of relying exclusively on text-based communication, schedule video or audio calls with close friends and family. Hearing a voice and seeing expressions provides a deeper sense of connection.
- **Limit Passive Scrolling:** Replace mindless scrolling with active engagement. Reach out to old friends, comment meaningfully on posts, and join groups where you can have discussions about common interests.
- **Mindset Shift:** Recognize that everyone, even those with seemingly perfect online lives, experiences loneliness and insecurity. Focus on building genuine connections rather than chasing a performative popularity.

The Importance of Quality over Quantity

True connection and belonging come from fostering deep bonds with a select group of people. It's in the shared vulnerability, the difficult conversations, the laughter and the tears that a sense of true community is built.

Here are a few tips to cultivate deeper connections:

- **Be Present:** When spending time with others, put your phone away and give your full attention. Listen actively, show genuine interest, and make an effort to deepen the conversation.
- **Initiate:** Don't always wait for others to reach out. Take the initiative to suggest meetups, organize activities, and extend heartfelt invitations.
- **Embrace the Awkward:** Building meaningful relationships takes time, effort, and sometimes a bit of awkwardness. Don't be discouraged by initial discomfort, persistence fosters closeness.

Social media can be a valuable tool to stay in touch and make new connections when used judiciously. However, it can never replace the richness, complexity, and fundamental support system that real human connection provides. By prioritizing in-person interaction, focusing on connection quality, and actively working against social isolation, we can harness the positive aspects of these platforms without sacrificing our deep-seated need to belong.

THE RISE OF DIGITAL DEPRESSION

The vibrant filtered photos, carefully crafted statuses, and curated success stories on social media often belie a hidden struggle. There's a growing body of research indicating a strong association between excessive and problematic social media use and an increased risk of depressive symptoms. While a clear causal link is still debated, it's undeniable that social media platforms can create fertile ground for low mood, feelings of hopelessness, and a pervasive sense of dissatisfaction, collectively termed "digital depression."

Unraveling the Connection

The relationship between social media and depression is complex and multifaceted. Here's how these platforms can subtly chip away at our mental health:

- **The Unrealistic Ideal:** Constant exposure to curated portrayals of perfect lives, bodies, and experiences fuels dissatisfaction with our own seemingly less glamorous reality. This perpetual comparison erodes self-esteem and cultivates feelings of inadequacy.
- **The Highlight Reel vs. Real Life:** Social media feeds present an endless parade of positive life events while obscuring everyday struggles, disappointments, and the sheer mundanity of existence. This distorted view reinforces a sense that we're constantly falling short or somehow missing out.
- **Social Isolation and Loneliness:** Even with hundreds of "friends," excessive time spent on social media can exacerbate feelings of loneliness and social disconnection.

Superficial online interaction cannot replace the depth, support, and shared experiences of true, face-to-face relationships.

- **Sleep Deprivation:** Late-night scrolling, blue light exposure, and anxiety induced by social media disrupts healthy sleep patterns. Sleep deprivation significantly amplifies negative moods, irritability, and depressive symptoms.
- **The FOMO Trap:** Witnessing others' social gatherings and exciting life updates without being part of them intensifies FOMO (fear of missing out). This fuels feelings of exclusion, anxiety, and fuels the urge to obsessively monitor updates that ultimately make us feel worse.
- **Cyberbullying and Harassment:** The anonymity and reach of social media emboldens online cruelty. Experiencing cyberbullying, hurtful comments, or public shaming significantly raises the risk for anxiety, depression, and even suicidal thoughts in vulnerable individuals.
- **Addiction and Loss of Control:** The dopamine-fueled reward system tied to likes, comments, and notifications can create a type of behavioral addiction, making it difficult to regulate social media use. This loss of control and preoccupation leads to missed real-life experiences and a sense of powerlessness.
- Doomscrolling: Compulsively consuming negative news and distressing social media content reinforces negative thought patterns, fuels catastrophic thinking, and leads to a pervasive sense of helplessness and hopelessness.

Who's Most at Risk

While anyone can experience mood dips due to social media, certain populations are particularly vulnerable to the development of digital depression:

- **Young People:** Adolescents and young adults, still developing their identity and sense of self, are especially susceptible to comparison-induced low self-esteem.

Increased susceptibility to peer pressure, heightened FOMO, and greater cyberbullying exposure put them at greater risk.

- **Those Predisposed to Mental Health Issues:** Individuals with pre-existing anxiety, depression, or low self-esteem are more likely to fall into negative social media usage patterns. The platforms can amplify existing insecurities and trigger depressive spirals.

- **Individuals Going Through Difficult Times:** Life transitions, such as job loss, breakups, or isolation can make people more vulnerable to seeking validation or connection online. Social media can become an unhealthy coping mechanism, worsening rather than improving their emotional state.

Signs of Digital Depression

Recognizing the signs of digital depression is the first step towards addressing this growing issue. Pay attention if you experience:

- **Persistent Low Mood:** Feeling sad, empty, or hopeless for extended periods.
- **Loss of Interest:** Apathy towards previously enjoyable activities, hobbies, or social interactions.
- **Social Withdrawal:** Spending increasingly more time online and less time engaging in real-world activities, particularly face-to-face connections.
- **Irritability and Restlessness:** Feeling easily agitated, short-tempered, or unable to relax, often fueled by social media-induced anxiety.
- **Disrupted Sleep:** Difficulty falling asleep, staying asleep, or experiencing a shift in sleep patterns linked to social media use.

- **Reduced Self-Esteem:** Feeling inadequate, unattractive, or unsuccessful, particularly when fuelled by social comparison.
- **Difficulty Concentrating:** Trouble focusing on work, school, or daily tasks due to social media distraction or rumination on online interactions.

Breaking Free and Finding Balance

If you find social media negatively impacting your mood and overall well-being, it's time to reset your relationship with these platforms. Here's how to break the cycle:

- **Be Mindful of Your Triggers:** Pay attention to which platforms, accounts, or types of content trigger negative emotions. Unfollow, mute, or reduce your exposure to these specific triggers.
- **Social Media Audits:** Periodically audit your social media use. Notice how your mood is impacted before, during, and after engaging with certain platforms.
- **Time Limits and Tech-Free Zones:** Use app timers to limit your time on social media. Designate tech-free zones in your home (like your bedroom) and times of day (mealtimes, an hour before bed) where you disconnect completely.
- **Curate a Positive Feed:** Fill your feed with accounts that uplift, inspire, or educate you. Actively seek out content that promotes self-acceptance and a balanced perspective.

Additional Resources:

If you experience persistent low mood, hopelessness, or any other mental health concerns, seek professional help. Therapy and/or medication can provide effective treatment and help you develop healthy coping mechanisms.

Social media can be a powerful force in the modern world. Understanding its impact on our mental health is key. Let's harness its positive aspects, mitigate its dangers, and ensure these platforms serve rather than silently undermine our well-being.

MINDFULNESS AND THE DIGITAL RESET

In our always-connected world, finding moments of true stillness and mental clarity is a radical act of self-preservation. Mindfulness, the practice of intentionally focusing on the present moment with openness and non-judgment, offers a powerful antidote to the incessant clamor and comparison traps of social media. Embracing mindful practices can help us reclaim control over our attention, reduce the mental chatter fueled by online negativity, and cultivate a greater sense of peace amidst digital chaos.

What is Mindfulness?

Mindfulness is more than just a buzzword. It encompasses these key elements:

- **Present-Moment Awareness:** Actively noticing the sensations, thoughts, and emotions happening in the present moment, without getting carried away by them.
- **Non-Judgmental Acceptance:** Observing our inner experiences with openness and curiosity, rather than harsh self-criticism or avoidance.
- **Intention:** Consciously choosing to bring our attention back to the present moment, even when our mind inevitably wanders to worries about the past or future anxieties.

Mindfulness is a skill that strengthens with practice. It's about becoming an observer rather than a constant reactor to the barrage of thoughts, feelings, and external stimuli vying for our attention.

How Mindfulness Combats Social Media Mindlessness

Here's how mindfulness practices specifically address the negative impacts of social media:

- **Breaking the Comparison Cycle:** Mindfulness helps us recognize comparison-induced insecurities simply as thoughts, not as objective truths. It fosters self-compassion and counters the envy or inadequacy that social media can stir up.
- **Rewiring the Brain:** Consistent mindfulness practice gradually alters neural pathways, improving our ability to regulate emotions, manage stress, and resist impulsive urges like reaching for our phones every time we feel discomfort.
- **Grounding in the Present:** Social media propels us into the past (regrets) or the future (anxieties). Mindfulness anchors us in the present, allowing us to appreciate simple sensory experiences often missed when plugged in.
- **Reclaiming Attention:** Mindfulness trains our ability to intentionally choose where we place our focus – be it on a task at hand, interaction with a loved one, or simply our own breath. This strengthens our cognitive control, making us less vulnerable to attention-hijacking platforms.
- **Taming Doomscrolling:** With mindfulness, we can notice and interrupt the negative spiral of doomscrolling with less inner resistance. We learn to reorient our attention rather than simply giving in to anxiety-driven compulsions.
- **Cultivating Discernment:** Mindfulness facilitates greater awareness of how social media impacts our mood, motivation, and behavior. This empowers us to make conscious, intentional choices about how we interact with these platforms.

Simple Ways to Integrate Mindfulness

You don't need to enroll in a silent meditation retreat to benefit from mindfulness. Here are simple ways to integrate it into your daily life:

- **Mindful Micro-Breaks:** Scatter a few moments of mindful awareness throughout your day. Focus on your breath for just a couple of minutes, notice the sensations of your feet on the ground while standing in line, or simply allow yourself to mindfully savor the first few bites of your meal.
- **Walking Meditation:** Take a break from screens and go for a walk. Bring your attention to the physical sensations of walking, the sounds around you, the sights in your environment. Let thoughts come and go without clinging to them.
- **Body Scan:** While lying or sitting comfortably, gradually bring awareness to different parts of your body, noticing any sensations of warmth, coolness, tightness, or relaxation. This simple practice helps release tension and grounds you in the present moment.
- **Mindful Use of Technology:** Next time you're about to open a social media app, pause. Take a few deep breaths, consciously decide how long you will spend scrolling, and intentionally choose the type of content you want to consume instead of passively reacting to your feed.
- **Mindfulness Apps:** Apps like Headspace, Calm, or Ten Percent Happier offer guided meditations, short grounding exercises, and resources to support your mindfulness practice.

Beyond the Individual: Mindful Tech Design

The responsibility doesn't solely lie on the individual to resist the pull of addictive design. Technology companies can and should integrate ethical considerations and promote mindful engagement with their products:

- **Friction Features:** Building intentional pauses into platforms – temporary freezes before endless scrolling can continue, reminders to take breaks, or prompts for reflection before posting a potentially inflammatory comment.
- **Transparency and Choice:** Allowing users to understand

how algorithms shape their feeds and providing greater control over the content they see and their time spent on the platforms.

- **Promoting Mindful Features:** Highlighting features that nudge breaks, encourage single-tasking, or offer moments of guided reflection integrated within the platform's design.

The Path to Digital Well-Being

Mindfulness is not a cure-all for the ills of social media, but it provides a potent tool to navigate the online world with greater intention, awareness, and self-compassion. By cultivating a mindful approach, we foster a healthier relationship with technology, enabling us to use it in ways that truly serve our well-being rather than letting it control us.

SEEKING OUT NEW MARKETS: SOCIAL MEDIA'S INFLUENCE ON CONSUMERISM

Beyond social, psychological, and emotional impacts, social media has profoundly reshaped consumer behavior, fueling an environment of constant temptation, manufactured desires, and the erosion of boundaries between social connection and commercial transaction. It has transformed the ways we shop, discover new products and brands, and ultimately how we define our own needs and wants.

The New Marketing Machine

Social media has revolutionized traditional advertising and marketing strategies:

- **Targeted Ads:** Algorithms gather vast amounts of user data, allowing for highly personalized ads based on our browsing history, interests, demographics, and online interactions. This relentless targeting makes us far more susceptible to impulse purchases than ever before.
- **Influencer Culture:** Partnering with influencers, from celebrities to micro-influencers with niche followings, creates a relatable and aspirational voice to endorse products. Seeing people we admire or identify with using and promoting items establishes powerful social proof and creates desire.
- **"Social Shopping" Features:** Features like Instagram's shoppable posts and "swipe up" links streamline purchasing. This removes friction and increases the likelihood of impulse buys prompted by eye-catching visuals and a fear of missing out on limited-time offers.

- **Peer-to-Peer Marketplaces:** Platforms like Facebook Marketplace and Depop facilitate buying and selling directly within a social network, blurring the line between social interactions and the potential for constant browsing and impulsive spending.

The Psychology of the Persuasion

Social media's influence on our spending habits leverages several psychological mechanisms:

- **The Need to Belong:** Advertisers tap into our desire for social acceptance and status. Products and curated lifestyles are presented as ways to attain a certain image, fit in with a particular tribe, or project success.
- **Manufactured Scarcity and FOMO:** Limited edition drops, flash sales, and influencer-hyped products create artificial scarcity and urgency. This heightens FOMO and triggers impulse buys fueled by the fear of missing out on something desirable.
- **The Illusion of Personalized Needs:** Algorithmically curated feeds create an illusion that the endless stream of products is tailored perfectly to our desires, even as these desires might be manufactured by the very platforms presenting them.
- **Social Validation Through Shopping:** Shopping becomes a way of expressing identity, with carefully chosen brands and purchases becoming extensions of our online persona. Likes and comments on our "hauls" further reinforce this behavior.

The Consequences of Overconsumption

Social media-fueled consumerism impacts us both individually and on a societal level:

- **Financial Strain:** Constant temptation and easy purchasing can lead to overspending, impulsive purchases, and mounting credit card debt. This is especially dangerous for young people with less financial experience.
- **Diminished Satisfaction:** The dopamine hit from a new

purchase is fleeting. This fuels a cycle of needing increasingly more to attain the same level of satisfaction, potentially leading to compulsive shopping and a sense of never having "enough."

- **Environmental Impact:** Fast fashion and the constant influx of trend-driven products contribute to a vast environmental toll – from resource depletion and pollution during production to overflowing landfills due to discarded clothing and gadgets.
- **Distorted Self-Worth:** When self-esteem becomes tied to material possessions and external validation through purchases, it erodes intrinsic self-worth and creates an unsustainable chase for fulfillment through consumption.

Resisting the Buy Button

Building a healthier relationship with social media-fueled consumerism requires a shift in mindset and conscious effort:

- **Question the Narrative:** Recognize that advertising and influencer content are designed to sell you a product and a lifestyle, not necessarily to improve your life. Reflect critically on the true intentions behind a sponsored post or tempting ad.
- **Unfollow the Urge:** Unfollow or mute accounts that primarily feature product hauls, lavish lifestyles, or constant promotion. Replace them with content that inspires creativity, promotes conscious living, or encourages experiences over material possessions.
- **Practice Before Purchasing:** Wait a set period (e.g., 24 hours, a week) before buying an item seen on social media. If you still want it and it fits within your budget after that time, make a mindful purchase rather than an impulsive one.
- **Embrace Secondhand and Sustainable Options:** Consider buying preloved items, prioritize ethically made brands, and support local businesses with smaller ecological footprints.
- **Find Non-Material Joy:** Invest time and energy into hobbies,

experiences, and connections with loved ones. These forms of fulfillment are deeper and longer lasting than the satisfaction derived from any purchase.

A Collective Shift

While individual changes matter, addressing overconsumption requires a broader societal shift:

- **Support Ethical Companies:** Choose companies with transparent production processes, sustainable practices, and a focus on quality over disposable trends. Make conscious choices with your spending power.
- **Focus on Experiences:** Encourage gift-giving that emphasizes shared experiences, homemade gifts, or donations rather than solely purchased objects, especially in relation to holidays and gift-focused events.
- **Advocacy for Regulation:** Support greater transparency in advertising practices, regulating targeted advertising for vulnerable populations like children, and promoting policies that encourage product longevity and repairability.

Social media isn't inherently evil, but its seamless integration with powerful marketing machinery demands vigilant awareness. By understanding how these platforms manipulate our desires and tempt us towards impulsive spending, we can reclaim control over our wallets, value experiences over possessions, and work towards a more mindful and sustainable mode of consumption.

DATA AS CURRENCY: YOUR PRIVACY ON THE AUCTION BLOCK

Lurking beneath the surface of every like, share, and seemingly innocuous quiz you take on social media lies a lucrative shadow economy. Your personal data – the likes and dislikes, friendships, locations, search queries, and even the most mundane of online behaviors – is a highly sought-after commodity fueling the multi-billion dollar data brokerage industry. This erosion of privacy has wide-reaching consequences that extend far beyond well-targeted advertisements.

The Data Collection Machine

Social media platforms and third-party data brokers amass an astonishing amount of information about you:

- **Every Click and Scroll:** Websites and apps track your every move online. They monitor what pages you visit, how much time you spend on them, the ads you click, and the content you share or engage with.
- **Beyond the Browser:** Many apps track your location, microphone access, contact lists, and other device-level data, building a detailed profile of your offline habits and interactions.
- **The "Free" Deception:** "Free" social media platforms don't come without a cost. The currency you pay with is your personal data, which they sell to data brokers and advertisers to generate revenue.
- **Connecting the Dots:** Data brokers aggregate data from multiple sources, both online and offline. This creates an eerily comprehensive profile of your interests, habits,

demographics, and even potential vulnerabilities.

The Billion-Dollar Data Bazaar

Once your data is collected, it enters a vast and opaque marketplace:

- **Targeted Advertising:** The most immediate use of your data is tailoring ads with almost laser-like precision. This makes advertising more lucrative for businesses and more tempting for you as the target.
- **Profiling and Prediction:** Data brokers create "digital profiles" on individuals. These profiles can categorize you by income, health conditions, political leanings, and countless other attributes, sometimes inferred even if you haven't directly shared that information.
- **Influencing Behavior:** With detailed insights into individual preferences and vulnerabilities, data-driven campaigns can nudge or manipulate behavior – from what products you buy to who you vote for, and even your core beliefs.
- **Data as a Commodity:** Packaged information is sold, resold, and traded among brokers, advertisers, and even governments. You lose control of who has access to your data and how they might utilize it.

The Dangers of the Data Trade

This erosion of privacy poses numerous risks to individuals and society at large:

- **Price Discrimination:** Companies can use data to predict your willingness to pay, inflating prices for services like travel bookings or insurance based on your perceived income or spending habits.
- **Predatory Marketing:** Data revealing vulnerabilities (e.g., gambling tendencies, health conditions) can open the door to exploitation by companies selling less-than-reputable products or services.
- **Employment and Insurance Impacts:** Insurance companies

could deny coverage or charge higher premiums based on predicted health risks. Employers could make hiring decisions influenced by potential biases revealed through social media activity.

- **Manipulation and Misinformation:** Bad actors with access to detailed psychological profiles can tailor disinformation campaigns, polarizing content, or even propaganda with frightening precision and effectiveness.
- **Surveillance and Suppression:** Governments, both authoritarian and democratic, can use collected data to monitor, track, and potentially suppress dissent, curtailing individual freedom and hindering accountability.

Protecting Your Data

Reclaiming some degree of privacy in the digital age requires effort and awareness. Here's how to minimize your digital footprint:

- **Audit Your Privacy Settings:** Regularly review privacy settings on social media platforms and apps. Limit what data they collect and who it's shared with, even if it means sacrificing some convenience features.
- **Think Before You Share:** Be mindful of what you post, like, and share. Once it's out there, it's difficult to claw back, and seemingly trivial information can be used to paint a detailed picture of your life.
- **Use Privacy-Focused Tools:** Utilize privacy-focused search engines like DuckDuckGo, browsers that block trackers, and consider ad-blocking tools to limit data collection.
- **Limit App Permissions:** When installing apps, pay attention to requested permissions (like location, contacts, microphone). Grant only the bare minimum required for the app to function properly.
- **The Illusion of Incognito:** "Private" or "incognito" browsing

modes offer limited protection – it prevents your activity from being stored locally but doesn't hide it from websites, trackers, or your internet service provider.

The Need for Regulation

Individual efforts help but are insufficient in the face of an opaque and largely unregulated data broker industry. Systemic change is needed:

- **Transparency is Key:** Users deserve clear and easy-to-understand explanations of what data is collected, how it's used, and who it's shared with.
- **The Right to Opt-Out:** Meaningful options to opt out of data collection and sale should be available, not hidden behind labyrinthine settings or misleading disclosures.
- **Data Ownership:** Individuals should retain ownership and control over their data, including the right to have it deleted or request transfer to other platforms to increase competitive options.
- **Breaking Up Data Monopolies:** The dominance of a few tech giants amassing immense data power hinders competition and undermines user privacy. Greater scrutiny and potential breaks ups are necessary.

The battle for online privacy is an ongoing struggle between individual vigilance and ever-evolving techniques to harvest and monetize our most personal digital imprints. By understanding the trade-offs inherent in the free services we rely on and actively taking steps to protect our data, we can begin to reshape the power dynamic and ensure a digital world that respects individual autonomy rather than exploiting it.

REAL CONNECTION: THE ANTIDOTE TO ISOLATION

In the age of social media, we've become masters of maintaining a digital facade – a curated, polished, and often disconnected version of our true selves. Yet, amidst the multitude of virtual interactions and likes, a pervasive sense of loneliness hangs heavy. Social media, while promising connection, can paradoxically exacerbate feelings of disconnection and isolation. The antidote lies in stepping out of the digital realm and fostering the real, messy, flawed, and deeply human connections that sustain and nourish our souls.

The Illusion of Connection

Social media platforms offer the tempting illusion of perpetual connection, but these interactions often lack the depth and authenticity of true human connection. Here's why:

- **Filtered Reality:** Social media presents highlights, not the full spectrum of messy, everyday life. This skewed view feeds insecurity, comparison, and the false belief that everyone else is living a more vibrant, successful, and fulfilling existence.
- **Quantity over Quality:** Hundreds of "friends" or followers don't equate to genuine support or belonging. Superficial likes and comments rarely provide the validation and acceptance found in real, face-to-face interactions.
- **Lost Nuances:** Text-based communication lacks body language, tone of voice, and the subtle cues essential to fully understanding and empathizing with others. This can lead to miscommunication, conflict, and a diminished sense of connection.

- **Asynchronous Isolation:** The ability to respond on our own time creates a false sense of togetherness while we physically remain isolated. Spending hours connected digitally displaces time for genuine real-world connection.

The Irreplaceable Elements of Real Connection

True connection, the deep bonds that fulfill our social nature, cannot be replicated online. It thrives on these elements:

- **Presence and Shared Experience:** Being physically present with loved ones, sharing a meal, laughter, or quiet moments creates an intangible bond that doesn't form through screens.
- **Vulnerability and Authenticity:** True connection requires being seen, even our messy, imperfect, vulnerable selves. This is difficult to risk online, where performative perfection is the norm.
- **Non-Verbal Communication:** Picking up on cues from tone of voice, expressions, and body language allows for deeper understanding and empathy. This rich tapestry of communication is absent in purely text-based interactions.
- **Physical Touch:** Human touch, a hug, a pat on the back, or holding hands, releases oxytocin, a powerful bonding hormone. Science confirms that we're wired for physical connection, something digital interaction lacks.
- **Shared Experiences:** Building memories, overcoming challenges, or simply sharing time together in the real world solidifies bonds in a way that online exchanges simply can't replicate.

The Benefits of Embracing Offline Life

Investing in real-world connections not only combats social isolation but offers myriad benefits for our well-being:

- **Reduced Stress and Anxiety:** Face-to-face connection, laughter, and social support act as a potent buffer against stress, lowering cortisol levels and promoting relaxation.

- **Enhanced Self-Esteem:** Feeling seen, accepted, and loved in our true, unfiltered form builds a sense of self-worth far more powerful than any number of social media likes.
- **Greater Empathy and Understanding:** In-person interactions help us develop empathy, understand differing perspectives, and build stronger bridges across social divides.
- **Boosted Mood and Outlook:** Social connection releases mood-boosting neurotransmitters like dopamine and serotonin. Genuine support networks help navigate life's challenges, fostering resilience and a more positive outlook.
- **Cognitive Benefits:** Studies link strong social ties with reduced risk of dementia and a sharper mind as we age. Conversation, debate, and real-world problem-solving keep our neural pathways active and engaged.

Fostering Authentic Connections

Building deep, lasting relationships takes time, effort, and venturing beyond the comfortable confines of screens:

- **Initiate and Prioritize:** Don't always wait for invites. Reach out to friends, suggest coffee meetups, or simply a walk in the park. Make real-world connection a priority in your schedule.
- **Join Communities:** Find groups based on your hobbies, interests, or passions. Shared activities offer a natural way to meet people and build camaraderie over time.
- **Volunteer Your Time:** Giving back to the community is a powerful way to connect with others, foster empathy, and gain a sense of purpose beyond your own social circle.
- **Practice Active Listening:** Be fully present during real-world conversations. Put away your phone, make eye contact, and truly listen to what the other person is saying and feeling.
- **Embrace Vulnerability:** Share not just the highlights, but also your struggles, fears, and imperfections. Allowing yourself to be seen authentically creates space for true connection.

The Importance of Quality over Quantity

It's not about having hundreds of friends, but about a few close bonds with people who offer support, unconditional acceptance, and truly enrich your life. Nurture these relationships with time, effort, and open communication.

Social media can play a role in maintaining far-flung connections or offering initial opportunities to meet new people. However, the deep human bonds we crave are primarily fostered face-to-face, through shared moments, unfiltered authenticity, and the subtle, irreplaceable nuances of real-world interaction. Prioritize in-person experiences, make time for the people that truly matter, and rediscover the profound, nourishing power of genuine human connection.

DOPAMINE DETOX:
RECLAIMING YOUR BRAIN

In a world designed to keep us hooked, scrolling, and endlessly tapping for the next digital reward, our brains are engaged in a constant battle for our attention. The relentless flood of dopamine hits from social media notifications, likes, and engaging content can disrupt our brain's natural reward system and undermine our capacity for focus, delayed gratification, and finding satisfaction in real-world experiences. A dopamine detox can be a powerful way to reset your brain, restore balance, and break free from the grip of digital compulsions.

Understanding Dopamine's Role

Dopamine, often dubbed the "feel-good" neurotransmitter, plays a complex role in the brain:

- **Motivation and Drive:** Dopamine surges motivate us to pursue things that meet our basic needs or offer potential rewards (food, sex, novelty, social interaction). It makes these things feel pleasurable, reinforcing the behaviors that lead to them.
- **Learning and Habit Formation:** Dopamine reinforces connections between a stimulus, action, and reward. This is essential for learning, but also how habits – both good and bad – become ingrained.
- **The Problem with Artificial Rewards:** Social media, games, and other online activities are designed to provide a quick and easy dopamine hit. The problem is, our brains don't neatly differentiate between natural rewards (a nourishing meal, genuine connection) and artificial ones (likes, social validation, level-up in a game).

The Dopamine-Hijacked Brain

Over time, constant overstimulation of the dopamine system can lead to several issues:

- **Reduced Sensitivity:** Bombardment with high-potency dopamine triggers (likes, notifications, viral content) can desensitize the reward system. Real-world activities start to feel less engaging and pleasurable by comparison.
- **Cravings and Compulsions:** The brain, seeking those easily accessible dopamine hits, produces cravings for social media or other forms of constant digital stimulation. This can manifest as an inability to resist checking your phone, even when it interferes with other activities.
- **Tolerance and Addiction:** Like with substance abuse, more and more stimulation is needed to achieve the same rewarding feeling. This leads to longer sessions on social media, chasing increasingly shocking or stimulating content, and a dangerous addictive cycle.
- **Impaired Executive Function:** The prefrontal cortex, responsible for focus, impulse control, and decision-making, becomes compromised by dopamine dysregulation. This makes it harder to resist distraction, prioritize long-term goals, and think critically.

The Benefits of a Dopamine Detox

A dopamine detox isn't about eliminating dopamine entirely. It's a temporary strategic reset, giving your reward system a much-needed recalibration. Benefits can include:

- **Restored Sensitivity:** Time away from high-dopamine triggers allows your brain to regain sensitivity to the subtler pleasures of everyday life, making simple tasks, hobbies, and connections more enjoyable.
- **Reduced Cravings and Increased Control:** As dopamine pathways reset, those insistent urges to check your phone or scroll fade away, restoring a sense of agency over your

attention and behavior.

- **Improved Focus and Productivity:** When not constantly hijacked by the promise of digital stimulation, your ability to concentrate, sustain deep work, and complete tasks significantly improves.
- **Enhanced Emotional Regulation:** Less tethered to dopamine spikes and crashes, you experience greater emotional stability, decreased impulsivity, and a greater ability to cope with boredom or discomfort without seeking immediate distraction.
- **Rediscovering "Real" Rewards:** A dopamine detox encourages you to find joy and fulfillment in real-world activities, hobbies, connection with nature, and the present moment, fostering a richer and more balanced life experience.

How to Do a Dopamine Detox

There are varying approaches to a dopamine detox, ranging from moderate to extreme. Here's how to get started:

1. **Set Your Intentions:** What do you hope to gain? What are your biggest problem areas with digital stimulation? Having clear goals helps with motivation.
2. **Choose Your Focus:** Select specific sources of high-dopamine stimulation to eliminate – this could be social media, gaming, mindless scrolling, or even news sites that trigger emotional reactivity.
3. **Duration:** Start small. A 24-hour detox is manageable for most. As you become more skilled, you can aim for longer periods (weekends, multiple days).
4. **Plan for Replacements:** Boredom and discomfort are triggers for relapse. Have alternative activities lined up – reading, spending time in nature, creative hobbies, connecting with friends in-person, learning a new skill, or simply practicing mindfulness.

5. **Taper Off Gradually (Optional):** If a cold turkey approach feels daunting, gradually step down your time on addictive platforms before the detox to ease the transition.
6. **Enlist Support:** Tell friends and family what you're doing to manage their expectations and gain potential accountability partners.

Expect Some Discomfort

Initially, you may experience boredom, restlessness, irritability, or anxiety. This is your brain reacting to the withdrawal of the digital stimulant. Persevere and remember these feelings are temporary signs of your reward system recalibrating.

Long-term Integration

A dopamine detox isn't a one-and-done cure. It's about fostering healthier long-term habits:

- **Mindful Tech Use:** Reintroduce digital stimulation slowly and intentionally. Set tech-free times, use app timers, and be choosy about the content you consume.
- **Seek Real-World Rewards:** Invest in hobbies, passions, and connect with real people.
- **Tolerate Boredom:** Learn to sit with moments of discomfort or boredom without immediately seeking distraction. This builds mental resilience and makes you less vulnerable to digital temptations.

A dopamine detox is a tool for breaking the cycle of digital addiction and reclaiming control over your attention and behaviors. By giving your reward system a much-needed break, you pave the way for a more mindful, engaged, and fulfilling relationship with technology and, ultimately, with yourself.

STRIKING A BALANCE IN
THE DIGITAL AGE

Social media platforms have irreversibly altered the fabric of our daily lives, the way we connect, consume information, and perceive both ourselves and the wider world. The boundless potential they offer for connection, expression, and knowledge-sharing exists alongside insidious dangers—comparison traps, the erosion of privacy, mental health pitfalls, and an unrelenting assault on our attention.

The true heroes of this story will not be those who reject technology entirely, nor those who fall completely under the sway of its addictive allure. True empowerment lies in cultivating a mindful, intentional relationship with the digital world; one where we wield its power rather than being consumed by it. This requires active effort, a willingness to examine our own vulnerabilities, and a commitment to using these tools in a way that safeguards our well-being.

Here are some key takeaways from our exploration:

- **The Comparison Trap is Toxic:** Embrace your own unique journey. Focus on self-growth and use social media, if at all, for inspiration rather than fuel for self-criticism.
- **Mindfulness is Your Superpower:** Practice moments of digital disconnection. Be present in real-world interactions, savor simple pleasures, and cultivate awareness of how social media impacts your mood.
- **Your Attention is Precious:** Treat it as such. Audit your social media use and set boundaries. Single-task, eliminate distractions, and actively choose when and how to engage.
- **Protect Your Privacy:** Understand the data collection trade-

off. Adjust settings, be wary of what you share, and advocate for greater privacy regulation.

- **Seek Real Connection:** Social media can supplement real-world connection, not replace it. Prioritize face-to-face interactions, shared experiences, and fostering genuine, authentic bonds.
- **Embrace the Gray Areas:** Social media is neither inherently good nor strictly evil. Its impact hinges on how you use it.

Navigating the digital landscape is an ever-evolving challenge. By fostering self-awareness, prioritizing our mental health, and actively choosing how, when, and why we interact with social media, we can harness the positive potential of these platforms without sacrificing our autonomy, privacy, or well-being.

Let us strive to be informed, empowered, and intentional users of technology – shaping it in a way that serves us, rather than allowing ourselves to be reduced to products within its relentless engine.

As you close this book, I hope you feel equipped with a deeper understanding of the complex forces shaping your digital experiences. Knowledge, as they say, is power. The power to resist mindless scrolling, to protect your privacy, to prioritize real connection, and to cultivate healthy tech habits that serve – rather than sabotage – your well-being.

This journey of transformation is not always an easy one. Old habits die hard, and the allure of social media's quick dopamine hits can be a powerful temptress. Don't be discouraged by setbacks; change takes time and persistence. Be kind to yourself, celebrate small victories, and don't hesitate to revisit the strategies and insights within these pages whenever you need a reset.

Here's your call to action:

Take Inventory: Honestly assess your current social media use. Which platforms give versus take? Are there any you'd be better off without?

Set One Small Goal: Whether it's tech-free Sundays, no phones in the bedroom, or learning about your privacy settings, one actionable change is the starting point.

Share and Spread Awareness: Have open conversations with friends and family about social media's impact. The more we discuss the downsides, the easier it is to support each other in finding healthier habits.

Remember, the ultimate goal isn't to become a digital hermit. It's about striking a balance, harnessing the power of these platforms without becoming enslaved to them. Imagine a life where you engage with social media consciously, where your mind is clear and undistracted, where your self-worth is unwavering, and where genuine, face-to-face connections blossom. This life is absolutely within your reach.

Thank you for embarking on this journey with me. Let's continue the conversation, share experiences, and build a community of empowered, mindful individuals capable of navigating the ever-evolving digital landscape with wisdom and intention.